The Great Fire of London

Deborah Fox

www.raintreepublishers.co.uk
Visit our website to find out
more information about
Raintree books.

To order:
☎ Phone 0845 6044371
🖷 Fax +44 (0) 1865 312263
🖳 Email myorders@capstonepub.co.uk

Customers from outside the UK please telephone +44 1865 312262

First published in Great Britain by Heinemann Library, Halley Court, Jordan Hill, Oxford OX2 8EJ, a division of Reed Educational and Professional Publishing Ltd. Heinemann is a registered trademark of Reed Educational & Professional Publishing Ltd.

OXFORD MELBOURNE AUCKLAND JOHANNESBURG BLANTYRE
GABORONE IBADAN PORTSMOUTH (NH) USA CHICAGO

Designed by Joanna Hinton-Malivoire
Illustrations by Peter Bull Art Studio
Originated by Repro Multi Warna
Printed by South China Printing Company, China
ISBN 978 0 431 12331 8 (hardback)
ISBN 0 431 12331 4   (hardback)
07 06 05 04 03
10 9 8 7 6 5 4 3 2

ISBN 978 0 431 12337 0 (paperback)
ISBN 0 431 12337 3   (paperback)
13 12 11 10
16 15 14 13

British Library Cataloguing in Publication Data
Fox, Deborah
   How do we know about the Great Fire of London?
   1.Great Fire, London, England, 1666 - Juvenile literature
   I.Title II.The Great Fire of London
   942.1'066

Acknowledgements
The Publishers would like to thank the following for permission to reproduce photographs:Bridgeman Art Library: p23; Collections: pp25, 27; Hulton: p24; Magdalene College, Cambridge: p20; Mary Evans Picture Library: p22; Museum of London: pp21, 26; Richard Thames: p4.

Cover photograph reproduced with permission of Bridgeman Art Library.

Every effort has been made to contact copyright holders of any material reproduced in this book. Any omissions will be rectified in subsequent printings if notice is given to the Publisher.

Words printed in **bold letters like these** are explained in the Glossary

Contents

Buildings that tell stories

This building in London is over 300 years old. It survived the Great Fire of London in 1666 when other buildings close to it did not.

This is a model of how London streets looked at that time. Can you imagine how quickly a fire would spread? This book tells you how the Great Fire started all those years ago.

The smell of smoke

Thomas Farynor was a baker who lived in Pudding Lane in London. Early in the morning on 2 September 1666, he and his family were woken by one of their workers.

The worker could smell smoke. A fire had started! The fire soon spread and the flames became so fierce that it was impossible to escape down the stairs.

Making their escape

Throwing open an upstairs window,
the family climbed on to their roof.
The flames were getting stronger and
they had to escape. Bravely they jumped
on to the roof of a neighbour's house.

Their maid was too frightened to climb on to the roof. The smoke was getting thicker. Sadly, she died in the burning house.

Too late!

It had been a very hot summer that year. The wooden buildings were so dry and they were so close together that it was easy for the fire to spread. The flames soon leapt from house to house.

A few hours later the fire was out of control. The Lord Mayor was in charge of fighting fires in London. But by the time he arrived, it was too late.

Panic

Buildings crashed down. Thick black smoke hung over the city. Frightened people tried to escape. Some headed for the boats on the River Thames. Others fled by horse and cart.

Some people did not have the money to pay for a boat or cart. They **sheltered** in the cool, dark stone buildings, which would not catch fire.

The force of the fire

People tried to put the flames out using **squirts** and buckets of water. They also pulled down buildings with **firehooks** to try to stop the fire from spreading.

It was no good. The fire was too powerful. The King decided that it was best to blow up the buildings closest to the flames to stop the fire from spreading even further.

The city in ruins

After four days the flames started to die down. The city was in ruins. People's homes and businesses had been burned to the ground.

Homeless people had to **shelter** under tents or in huts. Collections were made throughout the country to raise money for them.

The city is rebuilt

London had to be rebuilt. The King talked to **architects**. They said that buildings should only be built with brick or stone and that the streets had to be wider.

Gradually, over many years, London's ruins were replaced with new stone buildings on wider streets and with open squares.

How do we know?

Some writers who lived at that time kept diaries that tell us what happened. John Evelyn kept a diary and so did Samuel Pepys. Here are some of the words from Samuel Pepys' diary.

REceived the 26ᵗʰ day of *November* 1666, of Mr. *Thomas Lintott* returned from *Cowfold* in *Sussex* the Summe of *fifty three shillings & Nine pence* which was collected in the said Parish on the Faſt Day, being the 10th day of *October* 1666. towards the Relief of thoſe Perſons who have been great Sufferers by the late Sad Fire within the City of *London*. I ſay Recᵈ. by order of the Lord Major.

Sa: Kendall

This **receipt** tells us that the people of Cowfold in Sussex sent money to help the people in London who had lost their homes.

These Engins, (which are the best) to quanch great Fires; are

JOHN KEELING

This picture shows what the fire engines at that time looked like. They were very different to the fire engines we have today.

This picture was painted years after the fire. It shows people escaping by boat with their belongings.

New buildings for the city

This drawing is by Sir Christopher Wren. It shows his new design for St Paul's Cathedral, which was destroyed in the fire. Eighty-seven other churches and 13,000 houses were also ruined.

Here is St Paul's Cathedral today.
Does it look like Wren's drawing?

Objects and monuments

leather bucket

squirt

In 1666, there was not a fire service, as there is now. People used leather buckets to throw water at the fire. They also used **squirts** to fire water at the flames. They are very small compared to today's huge fire hoses.

This **monument** was built close to where the fire started. It was designed by Sir Christopher Wren.

Timeline

1am 2 September 1666 The Great Fire starts in the bakery in Pudding Lane, London.

4 September St Paul's catches fire.

6 September The King visits the people living in tents and huts.

10 September Sir Christopher Wren starts work on his design for a new city.

May 1667 House-building begins.

1671 Work starts on the building of The **Monument** to remember the Great Fire.

1672 House-building is completed.

1675 Work on St Paul's Cathedral begins.

1677 The Monument is completed.

By *1685* Wren has rebuilt 52 of the churches destroyed by the fire.

1710 St Paul's is completed.

1723 Sir Christopher Wren dies.

Biographies

Samuel Pepys

Samuel Pepys was born on 23 February 1633 in London. He was the fifth child of eleven and his father was a **tailor**. He studied at Cambridge University. He started to write his famous diary at the age of 27 but had to stop writing it when he was 36 because he feared he was going blind. Pepys died on 26 May 1703 at the age of 70.

Sir Christopher Wren

Sir Christopher Wren was born on 20 October 1632 in East Knoyle, Wiltshire. He went to Oxford University where he became a **professor** of **astronomy**. His greatest opportunity came when he was asked to redesign the city of London after the Great Fire. He died when he was 91 years old on 25 February 1723.

Glossary

architect a person who designs buildings

astronomy the study of the stars and planets

firehooks long hooks used to pull down buildings or parts of buildings that were on fire

monument a building or statue built to celebrate or to remember someone or something

professor one of the top teachers at a university or college

receipt a piece of paper that shows what someone has bought or given money for

sheltered hid from; found a safe place away from

squirt an early piece of equipment used to fight fires

tailor a person who makes or mends clothes

Further reading

Great Events: The Great Fire of London, Gillian Clements, Franklin Watts, 2001

How do we know about…? The Great Plague, Deborah Fox, Heinemann Library, 2002

Index